MAKING MOVIES ★

ANDREW WREGGITT ★

MAKING MOVIES ★

THISTLEDOWN PRESS

Canadian Cataloguing in Publication Data

Wreggitt, Andrew, 1955-
    Making movies

        Poems.
        ISBN: 0-920633-65-X

I. Title.
PS8595.R455M3 l989   C811'.54   C89-098069-1
PR9199.3.W745M3 1989

Book design by A.M. Forrie
Cover photo by Zach Hauser
Car by Dodge

Set in 10-point Garamond by Thistledown Press Ltd.

Printed and bound in Canada by
Hignell Printing Ltd., Winnipeg

Thistledown Press
668 East Place
Saskatoon, Saskatchewan
S7J 2Z5

Acknowledgements

Many of these poems have appeared in one form or another in: *Antigonish Review*, *blue buffalo*, *Canadian Broadcasting Corporation* ("Speaking Volumes", "Alberta Anthology"), *Canadian Forum*, *Canadian Literature*, *Dandelion*, *event*, *Garden Varieties* (anthology), *NeWest Review*, *North Coast Collection*, *Poetry Canada Review*, *Waves*, *Secrets from the Orange Couch*.

A grant from the Alberta Foundation for the Literary Arts allowed me the time to complete this book. Thank you.

Thanks also to Erin, Ann sensei and the Brisco Ridge Farm.

This book has been published with the assistance of The Canada Council and the Saskatchewan Arts Board

*This book is for my mother, Margaret Wreggitt,
and the memory of my father, Jerry Wreggitt.*

MAKING MOVIES

MAKING MOVIES ★

BURNING MY FATHER'S CLOTHES ★

*how long it takes to believe the
simplest facts of our lives—
that certain losses are final,
death is one, childhood another*

- Philip Levine

The Photograph:

If there was a photograph of that moment,
you would see
a boy about seven years old
He is wearing jeans and a short-sleeved shirt,
the yellow diamonds on his brown socks
descend like stars
into black and white sneakers
The boy is lying on an orange couch,
in front of him is a blank television screen
and slightly to the left,
a radio with lighted numbers on the band
The boy is listening intently to something,
hands cupped behind his head,
elbows pointed out
To one side, you might notice
a shadow falling over the arm-rest of the couch
The shadow is faint and barely
visible to the camera
but it is also part of the picture

What You Cannot See:

The boy is listening to a boxing match
between Cassius Clay and Sonny Liston
He doesn't know who the fighters are,
that they are in another country
or even that they are fighting each other for money
He has stumbled upon them by accident,
attracted by the frenetic announcers
and the rumble of the crowd
The boy is not listening to a fight
between two people,
he is imagining two names,
Cassius Clay and Sonny Liston

He feels the two c's of Cassius Clay
raking the bright, round sun
of Sonny Liston
He has imagined himself as the sound
of Sonny Liston, the sibilance of the s's
and the long oh's
He is suddenly tense and anxious
the way he often is at school,
the vowels of his silences, inarticulate
the sibilant shouts of children
The same moment, Sonny Liston staggers against the ropes
in the sixth round at Miami Beach
The boy feels himself pressed onto the orange couch
by a sound, the idea of Sonny Liston,
the sound of his name being knocked down
through the boy, this row of lights and numbers
The boxer raises both hands to his head
and leans forward with a body shot
What you cannot see:
The shadow that falls on the arm of the couch
belongs to the boy's mother
She has approached from the next room,
the hall light casting only a dim shadow
in the early evening
She is tired and has been waiting
for her husband to come home,
looking out the window
for the turn of his headlights
She is about to speak
as her shadow touches the frame of the picture
but there is a shout from the radio
and she stops to listen, her eyes fixed
on the face of the small boy, rigid, drained
Sonny Liston reels to the canvas

After:

The woman moves easily
across the space where the photograph
might have been,
her shadow sliding quickly across the room
to the boy's face
She gathers him up from the orange couch
her body blocking the hysterical radio,
cutting off the small lights and numbers
She is glad to feel the boy's arms
around her neck
The moments are pushed ahead,
lifted from the orange couch
The porch light is flicked on,
a flash of headlights in the driveway
Sonny Liston spits out his mouthpiece
and refuses to answer the bell for the seventh round
The boy lies in his soft blankets
nearly asleep, saying Sonny Liston's name
over and over in his head,
the small lights of the radio
burning like phosphorous
in his memory

russian thistle
dandelions
sweet, deep clover

The dog pushes his muzzle through
long grasses sweeping past his ears
shhh shhh
His tail swoops in the air
while the rest of him tunnels
in the thick leaves, thick smell,
his nose, a small wind
against the ground

A fat, striped bee lands
like a Boeing on the fireweed
and the stalk leans, tremulous
This kingdom of ditches, hums
in its cracked clay and dust,
under the low sky

horse tails
pigweed
morning glory

When I was half as tall,
I burrowed in weedy, vacant lots
The day so vast, morning and evening didn't exist
from the low hill of noon,
each day, its own field to be lost in,
with wasps and ants and sometimes
in August
a Monarch butterfly hovering for a moment,
laying its blessing on us

If I were to nuzzle down now in the clover and crabgrass,
I could not bring back that stunning expanse
of being young and closer to the ground,
of walking in the proximity
of the earth's own angels,
to smell these weeds so sweetly

pea-vine
marigolds
milkweed

The dog rubs his heavy fur
into the wild oats and burrs,
the pollen of this whole symphony,
a thunderous chord
at the end of his nose
The bee bounces on a single petal,
then lifts off, heavy, sated
The fireweed springs back, purple

Up here on the road, the human
stands in his fourth decade,
holding a few grains of memory
Up here in the stratosphere
of adulthood,
nearly six feet off the ground,
having grown up they say
But he is thinking perhaps

the limitless
the odour that drifts without memory
in and out of pink lungs
Nothing is like anything else,
everything is only what it is
astounding

This was the starry field,
a black curtain with tiny holes,
where we spilled out
of our young lives
How old were we? Six, eight?
We made movies, only better
than movies, because they happened
Actors and characters at once,
we pushed toward the bright
pinholes of light
Our pure faith was a curtain
hung from the rafters,
the half light and dust
of the neighbour's basement
Moments held shining like
bright coins
No, not like coins,
like stars we climbed through
into ourselves,
the intimate touch
of the black curtain,
smell of mothballs
The night was ours to put up
or tear down,
leave crumpled on the concrete floor
How we came alive
suddenly
anywhere in the universe!

These were serious times,
our simple language, small enough
to push through the dark curtain,
the baffles and props of school,
television, lunch with Campbell's soup
The good readers got
red and gold stars,

wore them like tiny badges,
on their tongues, the sour taste of glue
In our books,
Dick and Jane's mother
sewed the generations together
and their father drove
out of state even in Canada
The world, a place
where everyone was the same

We sat in our rows
and the sky grew smaller,
learned to imitate, with words,
sewing shut the holes of our belief,
trusting in our red and gold stars,
pinholes of knowledge
from which no light escaped

CARS

Driving with my father in Vancouver
the summer before he died,
the city's hum and exhaust
laying its warm hands on us,
the breath of the city
with its radios and going-home promise
The traffic grinds
like a slow metallic animal
undulating on its narrow track,
all of us trusting it
to take us anywhere, unknowing,
the animal we belong to

In our family, there was a different car every week
Sometimes cars only lasted
a day before my father sold them
Chryslers with flying tailfins,
or Mustangs with tail lights
like puzzled clown faces
brightening at the end of the driveway
Mostly, they were plain Ford Fairlanes,
Comets and Galaxies,
trade-ins that still held traces
of other families, other children
gawking out back windows
I investigated each one
when it came home,
opening and closing doors,
wondering always if this was the car
that would stay,
the car that would sit in the driveway
every weekend,
the one I would recognize
on the street, driving past,
my father in his suit
and hat just so

I envied the cars of my friends
whose parents came and went in them
with regular hours,
my friends who could say
"this is our car"
and all that went with that,
the ownership,
the security of a large object
always there in the driveway
As if it was a dog,
as if it could love you back

My father smiles as we ride
in the mechanical river, gears and tires,
each with its singular cargo
My home, the city I believed
was somehow different, wiser
than the one I grew up in
Still not understanding,
all those years, my father refusing to be defined
by the technology that drove us,
the pile of metal in the driveway,
recognizing the current that sweeps us
as human, not metal and rubber
Only now, I realize this is my last
image of him, leaning back in the passenger seat,
window open, the blare of summer heat
The imperfect machine of memory
we bring home to our own families,
the traces of love we search for,
opening and closing its gentle doors

DREAM

Black knot of Hutterites
stooped in the hot wind,
bent grasses, prairie wool
tilting wildly off the horizon
A young girl standing alone,
rooted in the turned earth
Out here, you must surely dream yourself
a black shadow in the hard light,
an aberration of geometry
under the pin-scrawl of jet-stream
Circles and squares
the plough writes on the earth
You must dream yourself
the black centre,
your print skirt and black boots,
the illusion of yourself
motionless under the eye of God

Like the Hutterite girl I saw
when I visited this colony years ago
Long halls where women
sat elbow to elbow and peeled potatoes,
their red gnarled fingers, scoured
The men returning from the fields,
tractors coming home through the dust
like an armoured division
bringing their beards, silent hunger
to the huddle of buildings,
their serious children, bowed heads in the gravel
In the centre of the village,
a platform with a hook and long pole,
a gallows
where pigs were hung and bled
This was the image I could not forget,
the still, empty platform,
the unforgiving wind

Years later, a pig hung there
in my mind, its throat cut,
thrashing in the blowing dust,
the solemn black coats rustling
But this is not what I saw,
it is what I dreamed,
thinking of the young girl
standing alone by this killing ground,
her face as blank and white as milk
She did not speak, only watched,
not just centuries between us
but the giant weight of a single dream,
the dream that is written on the earth,
words that are never uttered

It is in my own dream
that I see your face,
kerchief, the flat blue of your eyes,
a huge silence between us,
your words broken and ploughed
back into the soil
It is in my own dream
that I see you across this empty space,
this loss of words, hook and pole
where the bleeding pig will hang

The call, coming as it did, in the middle
of the night,
a sudden voice outside our tent,
a man's voice that seemed to rise
sharply out of this dream we were sharing,
the slapping of the creek,
the moon flat through the canvas,
                              permeable
Coming as it did, with a nervous
shuffling of boots,
                              opening
into the voices of other men murmuring by a campfire,
collecting flashlights, choosing partners

The little girl gone since late afternoon

A woman putting on coffee,
another clutching a small sweater
and looking up into the blackness,
as if the veiled dark could be parted by force
of will,
by the long white bone of her longing
My own mother shutting me into the tent
with the force of her voice   thrown
across the gravel from the campfire
nervous and quick

I heard the calling of men far off in the trees
and the solemn, hushed moving of others
just beyond the canvas,
in the wide-awake dark
Thinking of the little girl in the trees,
closed up like a pine cone,
the moon falling behind the mountain, extinguished,
the two of us caught in the same memory,
its slow unfolding

The call, coming as it did, out of nothing,
disembodied and urgent
when she heard it too,
her name suddenly there beside her

The way we share this even now,
twenty-three years later, grown up
and found
Even in the trees off the highway,
low sky of branches by the Liard River
where that voice still lives in a descending

                        pattern
            of sound waves
The small warm spot where the child lay down
and gave up her fear for a moment,
still warm with that presence
Something that is set in motion
and does not stop,
              the call
coming as it did

How we were picked up and held, both of us,
in those last few black moments
before dawn, by our relieved
and haunted mothers,
as the searchers slept uneasily
in the cold
absence of the moon

A rust-red rooster on the 52 Ford pick-up,
spurs clacking on the hot, blue roof
At my grandmother's house on the Black Water road
saskatoons and raspberries
grew like devilish children
in the oh's of bald tires,
spiky branches pushed
through the dust-caked fence
My grandfather working the old Caribou gold diggings,
a few flakes and nuggets, just enough
for flour and tobacco,
to keep the truck running
This is where I tumbled out
of the hot vinyl backseat in 1962,
cow-lick haircut, shined shoes
and stood beside my grandfather's yellowed grin,
his magnificently dirty hands
It seemed as though time
had fallen over on its side, laughing
and would not get up,
a red rooster cackling at the sun

Impossible to be out of place in this chaos,
to breathe here was to defy order
The young shepherd cross rummaged
in the tipped-over sluice boxes
and never grew bored
The yard filled with children
and neighbours, all of them drawn
to this place where people
ate when they were hungry
and later slept on the exploded mattresses
in the shade by the porch
At night, hands of rummy
dealt on the oil drum,
glasses of rye
and still no one went home

My grandmother shooed the cats
and sneaked cigarettes to my bigger cousins
The place full of lush greens
and loud plaids, my grandmother's
sandpaper laughter and cans
of Sportsman tobacco

How is it I've come to value
the familiar order of things now?
Like my parents of 1962, privately
discussing when we should leave,
reminding each other of appointments,
the house left untended, the long
drive home still ahead
Not possible anymore
to run with the half-crazed children,
to pan for nuggets in the worked-to-death creeks
and never consider leaving
How is it that in all this I remember
these two serious, young adults the best?
Talking in the half-lit kitchen,
having put everyone to bed it seemed,
their quiet words sparking
just behind my eyes,
mica in black sand,
their own childhoods stacked
like cordwood by the stove

Finally, even the dog
wanders home through the darkness
and the deep sleep of everything,
asks at the screen door to be let in
to this last bowl of light

Burning my father's clothes
in a metal drum behind the house,
my mother afraid to give them away,
afraid to see them walking by on a stranger
The oily black smoke coils
up through the trees
and out across the snow-covered hills

Here is the coat I remember
from the trip we took
to somewhere
I am lying in the back seat,
my mother asleep in the passenger side
Headlights flashing in his face,
he drives all night like this
in the silence of our sleeping
The world was safe and dark and intimate
His solitude with the white lines,
the flat prairie, the eyes of deer
sparkling in the ditches
and the dull glow of some city
still an hour's drive away
Waking up to see him there and I remember
even the smell of this coat, tobacco,
these deep closets of memory

Burning my father's clothes
The only child
standing in the snow and smoke and silence
I pile the shirts and jackets on
and the orange flames strike at them
over and over
The smoke billows up
and everything is given to the sky,
unwilling and stubborn,
ashes settling on the shoulders
of my own coat

The smoke sweeps through the trees
and up into the hills we worked together,
across the fence we built
And there is not a bird in this thicket,
no rabbits, or mice pushing through the new snow
Nothing moves or grows or mourns
for anything lost here
Only the smoke of my father's clothes,
spiralling up,
then falling in the cold air . . .

the face of my mother
anxious
hovering in the window

VISIBLE

I was out hunting with my father
Late in the year, very snowy
and cold
We had split up and arranged to meet back at the truck
As usual, I came back first,
cold fingers, toes numb
I hadn't seen anything,
not even tracks or fresh droppings,
as usual
I climbed into the truck and ate a sandwich,
peering out the window
After awhile, I just slouched down
and waited

I was tired and thinking about
how complicated it was to be fourteen years old
This problem about girls,
of being invisible to them,
one in particular
Also, thinking about that asshole
two grades ahead
who kept threatening to punch me out,
what that meant,
what I would do about it
if it happened
Sitting there hunched up,
dopey from all that walking,
going over things in my head, slowly,
this problem of being visible and invisible
to the wrong people at the wrong times

So, I was a little slow to realize
that down the cut line, way down,
at the base of the hill across the creek
there was something white
moving across the snow
Upright and striding, purposeful
I opened the window to look
Another hunter maybe,
but why dressed in white?
Then I realized how tall it was
in comparison to the power line struts,
ten or twelve feet
I got out of the truck
and put the scope on it,
got it centred just long enough
to confirm arms and legs,
leaning forward slightly,
very big and moving fast . . .
Then suddenly it's gone,
disappeared into the trees
Gone

My father came back to the truck half an hour later
and we drove home in silence
I don't know why, but I didn't say anything
about what I saw,
told no one until now
Maybe I thought it would sound stupid,
and even if it didn't,
what would anyone do about it?
Something big and white crossing a cut line
I was thinking about something else . . . not sure
what I saw . . . it's gone now anyway

We got home and there was
the warm smell of cooking,
steam from boiled potatoes
fogging the window
I went back to thinking
about tests and the asshole
and that girl,
what kept me fogged
and dopey and busy in 1969
Not interested in solving that particular mystery,
not trusting myself
even to believe in it
Fourteen years old
just trying to get by,
talk to a girl,
not get punched out

But for months, that white figure
would suddenly reappear in my mind
Big strides
disappearing into the trees
Less and less often as the years went by,
but still, even now it appears,
mysterious, like the first time
Something suddenly there,
big and white, moving fast
Something private and immense,
connected somehow to everything
and to nothing,
passing in and out of my life
without a sound,
for no good reason

You feel it is your right,
that you have been cheated
because I burned those letters from Russia
You think your heritage was lost to you,
that it was I who robbed you of it
What your mother has told you is true
I burned them all, every date and name they contained
and much more
I am not sorry, *mien Grottsehn*

You ask for what was never yours,
accusing me from your modern life
You feel it is your right
to cannibalize the past,
the dry bones of your ancestors
Perhaps it is
But first, listen
I can tell you this now because you are grown,
because there is no one alive from that time
At last, that suffering is over

Listen. The sorrow you would take from those letters
is not yours
It is not something you might find
at the bottom of a closet,
something to dust off and wear on your coat
What you want to know as history,
was to us the world groaning and dying,
was to us the terrible end of all we had known

Your mother could not have told you
that I wept as I burned those letters,
the horses pulling slower and slower
on the road back from town

Past the church, the fields
of our neighbours, wheat murmuring,
meadow larks in the ditches
    Strange to have heard those sweet voices
    as I read those words,
    terrible words...
        tou schlemm

The letters were a catalogue of the dead
Our families, our neighbours in Russia
murdered by the Bolsheviks,
tortured or simply taken away,
not seen again . . .
Helen, Martin, Henry,
Sarah, who sang so beautifully,
her voice like an angel's...
Isaac and all his brothers,
all their children . . .

These were not detached accounts
in the way you might read them now,
historical texts to be studied, analysed
I lived each event as I read of it
I knew each barn where a man was hung
for the crime of owning a Bible,
how the light fell through
the gapped planks of the stalls,
how the wind bent the crops in the fields where . . .
leva Gott . . . people slaughtered like livestock!
They were the lost of a family
such as you will never know,
Mennonite brethren, shattered seed of God

This is what I read in those letters,
the horror I could not release
    Slow plodding steps of the horses
    finding their own way
    in the dust and deep rutted track,
    the creaking of the harnesses

Each death was my loss,
each blow a wound in me
I looked up into the bright daylight,
beside me the little blonde girl, your mother,
who woke to the smell of burning paper,
who knew not to talk about the letters at home
Little daughter . . .

         tjlienit Schoptji . . .

Still, you want to know why
Yes, I remember the little boy with the questions, *Grottsehn,*
Do not be impatient with me
Understand that I burned those letters
because I had to . . .

> *Husband, you were the one who died in 1959*
>   *the lucky one*
> *You could not have imagined*
> *I would live for another thirty years*
> *Thirty years!*

> *At first, there were shock treatments*
> *in places with caged windows, prisons!*
> *The shouting all night . . .*
> *I curled up and stayed so quiet...*
>   *little lamb*
> *Later, there were drugs*
> *and then the homes*

> *Who would have thought there would be*
> *so many of us,*
> *crowding into the cafeterias*
> *like sick cattle?*
> *Banging our spoons*
> *on the shiny tables . . .*
> *The lost ones lurching in the hallway . . .*

My wife, Martha, was ill by then,
a disease of the mind
There is a name for it now, I suppose
To us, it was mysterious, unpredictable
She lived on the edge of a personal chaos
so dark . . .
the smallest thing would send her reeling
into that black world
A dusty plate,
a jar of milk gone sour
She would shut herself in her room
for days, her rage uncontrollable,
her depression
The children would whisper to each other
in the kitchen, afraid,
wondering what they had done wrong

How could I show her those letters?

> *I knew I was ill those years,*
> *   at least at times*
> *I pitied you, when I saw you*
> *sitting by the stove in the morning,*
> *   so tired . . . your hands curled that way*
> *There was love too, those*
> *tender moments . . .   nah yoh . . .*
>
> *But it was the girls I pitied most*
> *Like me, they had no choice,*
> *   they were born to it . . . this sadness*
>
> *I didn't choose this life*
> *I would have stayed in Russia*
> *if I could, with my family*
> *But I followed you, even though I was so afraid*
> *I thought my heart would stop*
> *I followed you and raised our daughters*
> *the best I could*

It wasn't always so
In the early years, she laughed so easily,
her head tilted a little to one side,
pulling her hair back, looking at me . . .
That simple motion filled me with such happiness!
Before we married, her family was all she knew
The world for her, for all of us, was no bigger
than the distance a wagon could travel in a day
I loved her very much and I believe
she loved me . . .
But we grew harder with the times
There was love of children,
love of God, but for us . . . *Zoh*

When the trouble began,
it was our families, people from our village
who made it possible to go
A few young couples sent to find land in Canada,
sponsor others
          But there were no others after us

We already had a small baby
when we boarded the train to Petersburg
Martha wept for days over leaving her family
and for the fear that possessed us all,
a cold, icy presence that never left her
There was so much to be afraid of,
the stopping and starting of the train
for weeks, the gunfire
in the forests around us . . .
Our first winter in Canada,
it seemed we had fallen
over the edge of the earth
Two families in a two-room sod house,
six children

The wind blew through the chinks in the walls
and the children were sick and hungry
Our baby cried all winter,
diapers hung around the stove
There were arguments and hard words
We were not wanted,
but who could blame them?
Everyone was so poor
At night, Martha would weep and whisper
that we should not have come,
even that God had abandoned us
Such was her sickness

> *I was a mouse, burrowed under the snow*
> *I nibbled my bread, suckled my young*
> *Outside, the wind swept over the snow,*
> *a Bolshevik horseman with no pity,*
> *cutting the breath out of me*
>
> *So I burrowed*
> *in my corner by the stove*
> *and never went out,*
> *dirt from the roof in my hair,*
> *my garland of soil*
> *I burrowed*
> *and let the days pass through me,*
> *one by one,*
> *like the shadows*
> *of the dead*

You cannot know the loneliness I felt
along those flat, dusty miles
            the stepping of the horses,
                the turning of the axles . . .
as I consigned each page, each German cipher
to ash

How I swallowed that ash at the supper table each day,
soup and bread, everything I tasted was ash,
bitter,
the ash of our poverty, our great loss
My wife and I, strangers to each other in our own house,
in the presence of our children

> *You speak of your loneliness*
> *but what about me?*
> *Most of my life spent in a cold, grey dream*
> *You have no idea what I saw*
> *in my worst times*
> *You speak of those letters*
> *but do you imagine I did not live through as much*
> *in my sickness?*
> *Terrible images that drove me crying from the table*
> *night after night?*
> *I knew they were dying,*
> *I felt us dying with them*
> *The deception at our table, my own daughters*
> *lying to me, afraid of me,*
> *my own husband!*
> *I did not want to know of those letters,*
> *I did not want to know!*
> *Still, I felt their suffering*
> > *and could not reach out*

Everywhere I looked along that road
were the tiny houses and blown fields
of others like us,
the countless, scattered children of other continents,
struggling for their lives,
for the lives of those who would come later,
for you, *mien Grottsehn*
What could I do, but hide my tears
from the little girl beside me
and carry on?

You could not have imagined
I would live for another thirty years
after all we had come through
A crazed, old woman talking nonsense
to the doctors . . . Shame!

I didn't ask for this, Peter
I didn't . . .
       ask . . .

Remember, husband
You brought me here
and then left me to grow old
alone

*Grottsehn,*do not ask for the grief I left
along that road
You remember a grandfather who built you
a wooden stool, who spoke softly to you in your bed
in a language you could not understand
An old man who died
before you even started to school

Be content, and don't ask
for the sorrow of others, the unhappiness and misfortune
of people you never knew
Let them rest
You can see them if you must,
in the lines and shape of your face,
your mother's easy laugh

Be content with that, *mien Grottsehn,*
          sie toufrehd
and look no farther

MAKING MOVIES ★

CROSSING THE DATELINE ★

We are chasing the dawn
across the Pacific,
flying through the day that doesn't exist
Our watches spin like haywire compasses
Meals arrive and are taken away,
we are roused like ruffled hens
from fitful sleep
Riders on the dateline,
hovering at midnight

I think of Mishima's images,
the separation of soul
from the moving parts of mind and body
Toru fixed on the horizon, watching
for the angel of himself,
his eyes reaching beyond
the Japanese haze, *maru* in the
distance
Precision, purity, the beauty that kills
I think of how I could have been the same
boy lightkeeper, so serious, so sure,
growing up in the cold, drifted
streets of Winnipeg
The boy who vowed to kill himself
if he failed
At what, he wasn't sure,
only his eyes fixed, unfocused
beyond the horizon
Maru, maru, calling in the haze

Tonight, there is only this horizon,
rows of tousled heads
nodding in and out of sleep
Each of us with a small
window of blackness,
each with our weariness,
our weaknesses and contradictions
dragged along like luggage,
lurching through the meaningless hours
And yet, some of us, finally
loved and forgiven, older
and less sure

Beyond our eyes, the gentle curve
of the earth falls away,
the sun waiting to ascend
like an angel

Imabari, Japan

The lion's mouth releases pigeons, flapping upward
Drums sing against leather tongues
It is the day men become the lion

They flash white leggings under the blue cape, wide
as the sea,
rippling with lion muscle,
this community of arms and shoulders
The creature they have become,
blossom, thunder, air
Deep in the lion's throat they invent
the power of flight,
their voices become colours
flayed out like pollen into the hills
These men of career ambitions, Toyotas
and company baseball

The lion rears
They stand on each other's shoulders
Stiff backs, erect, shuddering under the weight
of each other, this industry of muscle
At the top, small children ride
inflamed in the high, white song
One by one, birds are released to the spring sun

Untelevised, undefined
song of brotherhood, flesh and muscle
The pigeons settle high
in pine branches
All of them beating,
singular, startled
out of the lion's mouth
like the hearts of the newly born

K Orita

Rain hammers outside against
                              wide awnings,
tangles of bicycles on the sidewalk,
rain running through them,
crazy tablature up and down the street
Cymbal brush of tires
                              ssshhhh . . . ssshhh . . .
Coltrane drowning it all out or maybe
                              putting it together
Orita-san drums on the counter
                    Time
                              time café
Four tables and big stereo
He screws up his eyes, says he's going out of business
"Japanese people don't understand jazz" he says and
                    laughs, points at the speaker
                    Coltrane hitting high register, bouncing up there
                    beside the light fixtures
He says he'll go back to his parent's orange farm
and shrugs as
                    the bass solo walks a woman past
                    the window   syncopates
                                                        off
the curb
                    and around the corner, her
shopping bag going like this   back and
                    forth

He pours me a brandy
and one for himself
I think of the orange groves that line
the steep shores of these islands

Not so bad to work in a joy of oranges,
round and sweet
        like this note that comes swelling
        up from the speaker, ripe and full of
sheer orangeness against green trees
rising out of the red soil by the deep
blue blue water,
pleats of bright corduroy between
Honshu and Shikoku
The colours alone could sustain you,
even on a day like this
But Orita-san shakes his head,
he doesn't want to be "salary man"
even though I am his only customer,
a gaijin driven in by the rain,
even though the rent is too high
and the neighbours think he's nuts

So what?

There is something here
       subtle, between the notes,
       a door to the unknown,
       a kind of nourishment
         This long solo snaking out
around the counter, piling up
       the dusty bottles in a clump
       against the mirror, labels every
which way
I think of him walking in the orange groves
in his rubber boots, following a diesel tractor,
trying to keep the rhythms of Coltrane, Davis, Mingus
alive in his mind
while the monotonous
         chuk chuk
of engines
falls like the days of the week,

his albums and old speakers
in the dust and damp
of his parents' basement
       Time
            time

Orita-san puts on Charlie Parker, pours
another brandy and closes his eyes
To hell with the colour orange then,
the orderly groves and rubber boots
The rain outside lost in the riffs
of alto-sax, the door to the world
not opening all afternoon
He smiles, all his teeth showing,

      "Bird of Paradise!"

DOG AT ISHITE-JI TEMPLE

This dog is not a Buddhist
He is small and darts,
a minnow on thin haunches
Muddy grey over black and white markings,
the grime and soot of Matsuyama
on him like a mantle, an aura
He follows the ancient stone fence,
nose to the ground, lifts
a delicate hind foot
like centuries of venerable ancestors
When I bend down, he disappears
soundlessly into the sanctuary of lush green,
a single blur through the meditating rhododendrons
He has learned the ways
of beckoning children, old men
guarding refuse behind one-room cafés
Stones are for throwing,
the bowing of humans
not to be trusted
He has learned the escape routes of Ishite-ji,
the holiness of leafy cover
He does not care to honour the dead

A small, grey dog must be quick
in this world

for Mika Kono

Tough, hard language
of Mika's hands
                    here and
here
Mika, the blind girl
works on my knotted back,
Shiatsu,
American music on the tape recorder
Her seeing-eye retriever in the corner
watches like a Buddha
Slats of orange light
fall across the room,
fingers of sun moving
slowly across tatami floor
She wants to go to America,
to Los Angeles or Banff
"You are lucky to travel," she says

I want to tell her, yes,
but it's a simple travelling I do,
moving my body from one place
to another
Not like her,
hands that must travel everywhere,
not just the surfaces,
but into the secret spaces
between bone and muscle
Hands that touch my shoulder blades
and see that I am crooked,
leaning slightly
into the world,
an ache in my head

Hands that know this golden retriever
in the corner,
without ever seeing him as I do now,
fur gleaming in bars of light,
deep brown eyes on both of us

I want to tell her
America is like me,
a little tired,
a little crooked,
with an ache in its head
But the language I have
fumbles its meaning,
retreats into simple phrases
This language of images
that cannot show her
the Rocky Mountains, America,
or even the deep golden colour
of her dog resting in sunlight,
cannot soothe the aching
in even one person's head
America, for its music and strange clothes
longs to see as clearly as her,
to touch as precisely
the delicate centre
of its unhappiness

Wait. Don't speak
Listen instead . . .
Mika's hands here and
                    here
knuckles, palms
finger
tip
s

The night is a black flower,
a dull headache that blossoms
over the city
I lie awake and listen
to the rain-filled streets,
commuter trains shrieking in the darkness,
the two hundred thousand of Hiroshima
riding in the black smoke,
bearing their paper cranes
in the wet darkness

Here, old women walk hunched over,
backs fused
in a bleak question,
their spines twisted from a lifetime
in the rice paddies,
given to the nurturing of tiny grains
They push empty baby-strollers for support,
eyes forced down
to the striking of rain,
stooped now over wheels and axles
I imagine them tonight, in their beds,
curled into the shape of their labour,
the squeal of trains
lunging over them

In the parks, the twisted paper cranes
hang
and spin,
spin like the dead,
coloured paper folded
into birds without flight,
in this city of empty strollers

I lie awake and listen
in the shuddering of wheels and rails,
the voices of the two hundred thousand
calling in the black smoke
In this darkness, tiny lights
wavering in the mist,
what sleep is there for any of us?
For the old women who push their sorrow
in the streets,
for the millions we are, sorrowful
crippled with memory,
falling
like rain in the night

RYOKAN

Sometimes it is this simple
A Japanese girl in the bath,
the sound of water
moving in her hands,
her thin, high voice, singing
Each note carried up, mournful, longing
The intimacy of breath and steam

Sometimes, the delicate bones
of a girl's hands, wandering aimlessly
A single, wavering note released
through the thin walls of this inn
Delicate leaves in the garden
turn and turn in the light,
the stilled afternoon

Sometimes, it is this simple
A single listener carried up
in these motionless rooms
by the slow notes of a young girl's song,
by the loneliness we share
The child who is in us
and never leaves

Sometimes there is the single note
of our own youth
wavering in a closed room
The first cicadas of evening
beginning,
calling down the distant memory
of the stars

STRAW HAT

Imabari, Japan

A man is fishing
at the lip of the typhoon shelter
A ragged stick with straw hat,
a bit of cloth flapping,
an idea perched against the horizon
If I look down the length of my arm,
I can balance him on the end of my finger
against a backdrop of fishing boats,
ocean, islands, clouds, sky
In that order

Across the mouth of the shelter,
straw hat sees a blue jacket sitting
on the breakwater,
bicycle leaning on its stand
in the shadow of a warehouse
All this, he covers
with the brim of his hat

Straw hat urinates
into the water he is fishing in
What does it matter?
The land is only what the ocean
has thrown back
Somewhere across the world,
someone finds a glass buoy on the beach,
catches a glint of sun on the horizon,
thinks about getting home
Little creatures who scramble
at the edges of great oceans,
thinking about this
and that

All around, the rough cough
of two-stroke engines,
the squeal of winches in the tired shipyards
Straw hat, blue jacket squared off
in each other's vision
How much more do we need to know?
Here is a straw hat, here a blue jacket,
between them, Pacific Ocean
or thin stretch of water
They put each other in perspective
as the wind tears at their clothes,
as the sun falls behind
the shipyard crane,
as they both begin to consider their supper
In that order

MAKING MOVIES ★

THE LIVING   ★

Start with a saw,
broad-toothed, cross-cut
Cold groan of snow and mitts
blackened with grease, creased
palms, cigarette,
damp and bitten
on its yellowed end
Start anywhere
The 1930's in northern Saskatchewan,
monkey-wrenching the Model A
with scraped knuckles,
the hay-wagon axle
Work and sleep
turning each day over,
a piston rod, in the slow
cold, oil of winter
Cattle press their blunt noses
to the trough,
roll their eyes and bawl,
complaining as they crowd against spruce poles
Start with a stove that needs to be filled,
snow swirling up from the south,
the broken water pump,
the swollen porch door

Or start here instead
An old man in his garage,
laying out tools, socket set
in descending order
Half-inch, three-eighths
Screwdrivers, flat, Phillips,
biggest to smallest
An old man, fiddling
a stubborn jig-saw,
not coming in for lunch
when he's called
"too busy just now",
though nothing here needs fixing

A young man stands against
the bright doorway,
a shadow fallen out of the future,
sunlight drifted like snow
into the dark toolshed
"Your tea is getting cold"
The engine lugs, pulling itself
over, one piston
thumping slowly
after the other

This descending order of sockets, wrenches, saws

        Somewhere, cattle bawling in the night,
        hungry, pressing forward
        Or the spew of a storm blowing
        through thin, sagging fences,
        snow swirling on the horizon,
        on the edges of sunlight
        Pliers and hammer,
        cigarette clamped in stained teeth
        or balanced here on the work table,
        ash ready to

fall

Start anywhere

He probably smoked Sweet Caporal or Export A,
hand-rolled
On the new window ledge
beside him, a sealer jar of nails
scrounged from the alley

This afternoon, I imagine him
setting down his hammer
as he draws on his cigarette,
a little worried perhaps
about his family, this new house,
about building it in the 1930's
the depression settled over
the city, a black cloud
that threatens for years
but will not rain
Around him is the sweet smell
of newly sawn lumber, tobacco smoke,
simple orange light washing
across the river
In the low bushes,
a warm spring wind with its vague
promises, ruffling the hunched sparrows
He stubs out his smoke
and goes back to work
To fight the lethargy of these times,
hammer and saw,
you make your own lines pure
and true

Today, I smell the same warm
March wind, its hint of melting snow
out in the fields

I hear the builder's children
walking on his groaning floorboards,
descending the dark hardwood
stairway,
generations moving through
these walls,
my brothers and sisters,
decades of tenants
gone before
All of us the children
of one worried man,
a determined carpenter in a bad decade,
his jar of rusted, odd-sized nails
The slow halo of Sweet Caporal

This afternoon, I will take up the hammer,
choose my own measure
on these loose porch steps
The house settles
into the orange lap of evening,
the foundations sagged inward

but holding

i.

Out of the bush in 1915,
beat up from being yanked around
on the end of a crosscut saw,
from fighting those big skidder horses
in the blackflies and the wet,
clothes nearly rotted right off
The kind of camp where the foreman
puts his boots to you if you talk back
or get sick and refuse to work

Sixteen years old,
the end of his first season
Sault Ste. Marie, mud and early
wet snow on the streets
Like he's been released from prison,
hardened, sore,
glad to get the heavy caulk boots off,
to see the last of those grim faces,
those miserable sons of bitches
at the other end of the saw

In the train station, posters
for the war in Europe,
(Germans cutting off the hands of babies,
mothers being dragged by the hair)
He believes this is what's going on
The way he believes
a horse is the only way to skid logs,
that the Finn with the scar will kill you
if you touch his things,
that a gyppo show is the best way to make money
if you are young and strong enough to take it

the way he believes he is
young and strong
enough . . .

Exploded horses in the road,
the sucking mud on either side
The smell of carrion on the roof of his mouth

This handful of ragged German boys
shuffling through the smoke ahead of him,
rifle riding on his arm
dangling stupidly

In every direction, the land is peeled away
exposed, cavernous sores bleeding into the air
The road is falling off the edge of the horizon,
him on horseback, the Germans walking
The sky breaks open in flashes,
pushing them ahead
There is only one direction,
away

He wants to know about the posters
from up here on his horse,
herding prisoners two years later,
he wants to know if they lied to him
about this too

The boy with the black pits for eyes,
the boy who speaks English,
the blond German boy holding himself
together with what
remains of a dead man's coat
stops, his face turned up to the rider
and laughs
and says they had the same posters in Munich,
and laughs again, turning back

the road out ahead of them
believing in it,
in its hardness, its single direction,
moving ahead
as if they had chosen it

What he wants most in the world is a drink of water from the canteen strapped to his belt. He has been thinking of nothing else since he came to in this mud and din and stink.

The first bullet passed through his left forearm, shattering the bone near his elbow, and then lodging in the stock of his rifle. The arm lies beside him now in the mud, a torn, bloody sleeve.

The second bullet pierced his upper jaw on the left side, nipped off the end of his tongue and then exited through his right cheek. He knows it's bad. But he's not thinking about that. It's the water he wants.

Two problems:

The first problem is that he can't reach the canteen with his good arm and his broken arm is of no use at all. He has been lying in this shell crater for six or eight hours, slowly bleeding to death. He expects to die before he is found. As each hour goes by, he is more and more sure of this. What he cannot accept, is that he has to die thirsty.

All this time to think about the canteen on his hip and how thirsty he is. It's bad enough to be shot in the face and left to die in a stinking mud hole, but to be taunted like this, in his last hours, the canteen sitting right there . . . This is what he is thinking as hour after hour the shells explode around him, as the shattered, grey daylight sinks into darkness . . .

. . . so that when the wounded German rolls over the lip of the crater and down beside him, he starts in right away with his bleeding, ripped mouth, trying to tell him he wants a drink from the canteen. The German is in a bad way too, maybe dying. There is a terrible gaping wound in his side, but what Curt sees, is that he has the use of his hands.

Curt offers bandages from his first aid kit and keeps nodding toward the canteen, trying to form the word "wasser". Finally, the German seems to understand, he is nodding "yah, yah". He reaches over and takes the canteen off Curt's belt, slowly tips it up . . . Curt's eyes roll as his lips touch the metal top, straining forward.

He sputters a little, in what might be a kind of laugh, or a sob, as the warm, bloody water pours out through the hole in his cheek . .

This is the second problem . . .

GEORGE

i

It has not been easy to get here
It is winter and there is the danger
of slipping on the ice
Fifteen below and snow threatening from the north
(old woollen scarfs, thick winter undershirts, toe rubbers)
They are both over eighty years old, Tom and Curt,
they know what it means to break a hip
A grandson had to be called to drive,
a spare room made up, dusty bedding
hauled out of closets

They are silent as they walk, stiff-legged,
past the reception, the TV room, the cafeteria
They know it could be them next year
instead of their brother George,
if their health is a little worse
Long linoleum floors, flourescent lights,
the red exit sign at the end of the hallway,
where no one ever exits
It could be them staring from raised beds
at the wintry strangers
bundled in from the cold,
nearly forgotten outside
Red, watery eyes staring up from pillows,
surrounded in a clutter of photographs,
pictures of elderly sons and daughters,
unattended weddings of grandchildren,
a shot of someone's baby
taken last Christmas . . .

The view from the far bed,
a slanted rectangle year after year

ii.

They find him in a wheelchair
by an open window
His eyes and nose running, his body shuddering,
the wind flicking thin wisps of white hair
The nurse who has brought them here
runs to close the window
She doesn't know how this could have happened
another nurse's mistake perhaps, an accident

George's skin is milky and opaque,
a delicate sheen, like a fly's wing
Blood vessels lift out, a blue web
hovering near the surface
His shrapnel wound creeps
out the open sleeve of his gown

He will speak only certain words,
each one with a variety of random meanings,
                              associations
His eyes fix on an eyebrow,
                    a corner of Tom's jacket
He doesn't know who they are

Tom puts a blanket around George's shoulders
Curt twitches the white, puckered scar on his cheek
They stare at each other in silence
They know this is the last time they will see him,
that he will open the window again,
push himself into the stiff winter wind,
his lungs pumping, rattled and weak,
mucous rising in him like a tide

They are all over eighty years old,
these brothers born in a different century
They know, by now,
what is an accident
and what is not

It looks small here,
                    a narrow swatch of pavement,
mining town on one side, sweep
of treeline on the other
Poplars flutter this morning,
the wind rising off the lake
Behind me, a small brown house
pushed into a corner of its field,
                    having pulled its wheelless pick-ups
                    and crushed Datsuns close around
In the ditch, a dead mongrel
lies in the weeds,
small, black, its rib-cage swollen and legs stiff out,
                    paws crossed, saintly,
                    a halo of flies

This narrow line I grew up beside
where I waited for something to happen,
watching the yellow lines
that led to Prince George, Vancouver,
who knows, maybe New York or farther,
the future we thought was waiting for all of us
Believing when the time came,
we would climb into our rusted Toyotas or Fords
and push past these highway signs, finally,
                    a kind of secret music in us,
                    the last dull glow of the Chevron station
                    fading

Once, going to a party fifteen miles away,
six of us crammed in someone's car,

I opened the door to be sick
at seventy miles an hour, the pavement
gliding past, six inches from my face . . .
                    the soothing clatter of pistons, the tires
                    running and
                    someone yelling "grab him",
                    watching the yellow lines fly past . . .
All that wasted lemon-gin
in the humming dark

Who were those others, the hands that reached out
and pulled me back?
Some of them killed years later in twisted car frames,
some still leaning on hoods at the Chevron,
taking their anger up to the mine on the night shift
So many lost friends I hardly knew,
dreaming of Vegas, or Calgary,
                    listening for that secret music,
                    that deep longing

Walking this highway decades later,
this same thin, hard road,
having been where the yellow lines go
Above me, a wash of leaves,
and the small touching of the wind,
                    walking by the brown house,
                    huddled boneyard of wrecked cars,
                    this tiny bloated dog
                    who only wanted to go across,
                    the wind in its black fur,
                    and the smallest tip
                    of a pink tongue
                    showing

E.M.

Strange that I still count time by the years
gone from Vancouver
Five years since cherry blossoms
covered the windshield in March,
since I left Randy reading Jean Genêt
in that cheap hotel room, a bottle of whisky,
a cast on his arm
Five years, and still,
this morning I woke up startled,
closing his cheap veneer door again in my dream,
saying "see ya later",
then walking down the long, dingy hallway,
worn Oriental carpet and bare lightbulbs . . .
     I am thinking this by the stove
     as I make coffee,
     snowflakes drifting by the window
 . . . "see ya later"
and I never did

How many years since we followed the railway in the dark down
Arbutus Street, pushed the cork into a bottle of Sangre de Toro and
walked out onto the bridge crossing False Creek? Ha, ha, Sangre de
Toro, we laughed, as the one-eyed diesel stood poised on the
other
side . . .

Wait. Is this where it gets muddled up?

It wasn't me in the hotel room, it was someone else
Someone who took a picture of Randy and then gave it to me
His blond head beside the Wiser's whisky bottle, his cast
on the table like a loaf of white bread, the door behind him,
the same one I didn't walk through that day
into the . . .

And we didn't cross the bridge either, did we?
We turned back in the dark, the engine's light
shining over the choppy water, right at us
Not that crazy
Not that time anyway

Times like this,
I think if I fell backward
into these images
I would not be able to stop, I would keep ending
my life a moment at a time,
plummeting into the future,
trying to add up the irrecoverable
And nothing would change, or stay the same
And the coffee would probably
never get made

Some things that end
just go on ending, year after year
The image of Randy, his Wiser's and Drum tobacco,
opening Jean Genêt in a room I keep inventing
The truth or untruth of it
hovering beside my head as I make coffee five years later,
as I bring in the newspaper,
moving forward, slowly,
the first fat snowflakes of the year falling on the sidewalk like
blossoms

for Roger

High on the shoulder of the mountain,
past the deep pine forest
and the stunted gnomes
at the treeline
High in the wildflowers
and rock,
marmots singing in the rock walls,
Aristophanes' chorus
Wind ruffles
smooth arm of the peregrine,
curls off the cliff face
and brushes our cheeks
Urgent message,
a word spoken behind you somewhere

Did you say something?

You and I have been climbing a long time,
years, I think,
pulling ourselves over the stubborn shoulders
of our lives
As usual, we are a few paces apart,
walking into the wind,
thinking our city problems
that we take with us everywhere

But this mountain is not a life
or a metaphor for anything else
The mountain is busy with itself
The marmots sing only
for each other
The blue glacier across the valley
hangs on its lip of granite
for its own purpose

It is you and I who are climbing
That's all

What I wanted to tell you was,
it's alright to be up here,
locked in our separateness, to be
a few paces apart, as usual,
walking the same track again
after all this time
To feel these muscles pulling . . .

The wind, through alpine flowers,
the peregrine wheeling overhead,
like a word spoken
just behind you,
at the base of the neck

Did you . . . ?

for Susan

i.

Sparks fly up in the deep black
We shift on blocks of wood,
smoke pursuing us
Pause
                              between
words
Dog, muddy and panting
by the fire, thinks
the same thought
over and over

Montana river with its slow drawl
at the pool, eddying back on itself,
then down to rapids
Always drawn to rivers, you and I,
where we learn to speak, slowly
about the future, the present
We put our words into the fire,
watch them fly up
one at a time
Beside a thin reed of water,
invisible horizon of mountains

We imagine this,
each other,
in the circle of our fire

ii.

Overhead, calling of geese in the night
My chest aches imagining them,
blind birds, leading each other in the dark
Each sound fits the ear,
a sudden whisper
through all these layers of memory,
layers of darkness

> I can say it best out here
> out of context, or
> beyond context,
> in the pause
> Love is a word flying up
> between us
> over and over

Geese calling in the blackness,
in our deep memory
My chest aches imagining . . .
this instinct that leads us
precisely toward each other
beside any river,
in any season,
any darkness

THE LAWN BOWLERS

A woman stands posed, leaning
after her throw
Behind her, the others perch
white as gulls
on the thin brown benches
A man is speaking softly, his eyes
turned to the game
What he says is unimportant,
what is essential; the turn
of his white knit sweater,
the physical relation of wooden balls
against the immaculate green plain,
the deep blue of the sky
At the other end, a ball ticks gently
into the small huddle,
round black shoulders,
the single white heart

In the man's house, the furniture
is being sold
After eighty-seven years, he must exchange
his home with its intimate corners,
the joists he replaced himself
twenty years ago,
for a room in a stranger's house
He must choose the essential,
a television, a chair, a picture frame
Oh, never mind, give it all away
Memories hover close, intimate as breath,
the odour of flowers
A chair, a television, a picture frame,
small perfections,
routes out of the heart

The man keeps his eyes on the woman
tilted against the arc of the ball,
her arm outstretched,
wrist turned down
A courtly dance,
each of them leaning out precisely
toward each other,
a game of open palms
over the wash of green
The balls hug each other and whisper
never mind, never mind

The woman's arm drops slowly
She turns and smiles at the man,
his white knit sweater
and stooped shoulders
Small perfections of green
black, white
When they speak, their voices
are released into the air
like the simple perfume
of flowers

The balloon lifts with short
bursts of fire, nylon
expanded like a lung
Four people ascend the early light,
stand motionless in the air,
arms at their sides,
as if suddenly risen from a bus-stop
lifted above the city's grid
by this red and green flag
They move with each touch of wind,
the perfect calm of their perch
Only the earth slips away
beneath them, a lone walker,
face turned up, a curious
fleck of colour
in the brown grasses below
A shadow brushing over,
with its darkening breath

Another funeral last week,
the third in three years
Standing in our dark suits,
the freshly mown grass,
Wayne said, "You're supposed to be
a pallbearer twelve times
Six times for yourself and six
times for your wife"
Six good men, six feet of earth
Who has made these rules,
our lives finished with tidy sayings?
A body is lowered into the ground,
my own arms guiding its passage,
the same arms I hold up
to the sun this morning
to watch these nameless
riders on the air

When I have laid twelve of my own
into the earth,
who will tell me my work is finished?
A stranger commits us to the earth,
another washes our bodies,
another pronounces us dead
Who knows how the body's bones
crack in the still night,
the disease pushed through its brittle calcium?
How the hospitals tend the sheets and the televisions
while the bodies go their own way?
Who knows that our hearts were broken
years and years ago,
how we long to rise on the air,
our bones light and hollow
as a bird's,
our cries muffled against the wind

Twelve of my own
I dream always
of pulling these shadows
up into the sleepless sky

THE LIVING

i.

What he remembers:

Swimming like a fish on the hospital stretcher
He is laughing
because the water he is lying in
is so blue
A perfectly still pool
with himself at the centre,
a rolling salmon, crooked snout and stoop
of an old spawner, Tyee
He slaps his hands down to splash,
break the surface
He wants to dive under, through it
his jaws gulping like gills
He is swimming this way
down the hospital corridor,
the cool air rushing across
his naked chest
It would be funny as hell
he thinks
if he could tell someone
if he wasn't so busy
if he wasn't having a
                        heart attack
right now

ii.

When I go to see him, he says
The buffalo are gone. That's what started it.
There used to be so many,
they nipped off anything that dared
poke its head up.
Thousands of them, grazing on the tender
young sprouts.
This is all we talk about this day,
the lost prairie

He is almost ninety years old,
old enough to remember the flat prairie
of his youth,
unbroken and undulating in the stiff
westerly winds
Now poplars sprout everywhere,
old windbreaks run wild,
alders crawl out of coulees

Through a corner of the window he sees
delicate fingers of willow
waving to him
In his mind, he sees
wave after wave
of shimmering grasses

I help him to his feet
and he looks out the hospital window,
his eyes narrowed
The weeping willow flutters
in his face
He wants to see through the trees,
the clutter of green,
to the deep ocean of soil
he was made from

iii.

These days there are pills to take
Red and yellow and green
Chemical police,
they regulate the flow of life juices,
even the dynamite pill, the nitro
to blast awake his dozing heart

It is a quiet ritual before bed,
a glass of milk, a red pill,
a piece of banana, a yellow pill
In the glow of the fridge light
I pour milk, cut up the banana
For a brief moment, he stops,
his hand on the glass,
and his eyes dive deep
into that other place,
the place he has glimpsed already,
the stream he is struggling to climb
I stand there, holding open the fridge door,
waiting for him to come back,
to complete the small ritual of pills

In a moment, he will lift his eyes up to me,
up through the fine glitter of blue,
the still pool we are all moving through
He will surface once again
in the unfamiliar present,
the crowded, altered landscape
of the living